GRADUATION

INSPIRATION

2

AVONSIDE
PRESS

GRADUATION

INSPIRATION

2

More Inspiring Quotes from the World's Most Uplifting Graduation Speeches:

How to Escape the Hamster Wheel and Live the Life You Want

EDITED BY
ALISON WILSON

ISBN: 978-0-9942855-1-5

Avonside Press Pty Ltd
PO Box 174, Freshwater Beach, NSW 2096
Australia

The wisdom of the wise,
and the experience of ages,
may be preserved by quotation.

Isaac D'Israeli

Other Books by Alison Wilson

Graduation Inspiration 1

Graduation Inspiration 3

Hold The Phone:
The Definitive Guide to How to Protect Your Health from Phones and Wireless

Hold The Phone: Here's Why:
Advice from the Experts on How Phones and Wireless Affect Health

Websites:

www.holdthephone.co

www.graduationinspiration.com

Contents

Intro

This book is here to show you that your life doesn't have to be the way that you may think it 'should'; the way others have told you is 'best'; the way you've always assumed it will be.

There are many quotes here from people who have taken the time to try to show you that not only is there another way – there are many other ways to live your life.

When given the opportunity to speak they decided to be generous. Rather than simply talking about themselves – and let's face it, that's the way most graduation speeches go – they decided to share something that they'd found to be valuable. Something that they thought might be important to you too.

Many of them have talked about how life-changing it is to look at things in a different way; how breaking your way out of the status quo can be liberating; how critical it is to think about and define 'success' on your own terms; how 'failure' is often a stepping stone to something far, far more valuable than you ever thought possible; and how important it is to follow your own heart and passions, rather than simply blindly following someone else's footsteps.

All in all, they offer you a recipe for freedom. A way to step off the treadmill. What they're offering you is a blueprint - showing you how to lead a life less ordinary.

"Your time is limited, so don't waste it living someone else's life."

Steve Jobs

What They've Got To Say:

The Quotes

Overcoming Fear

Don't be afraid of fear.

Because it sharpens you; it challenges you; it makes you stronger.

And when you run away from fear, you also run away from the opportunity to be your best possible self.

Ed Helms
Knox College 2013

For me, the insight that has personally helped me the most when dealing with fear has been to understand that fear is primarily a creation of the mind.

I create it in my mind - it doesn't really exist outside the mind. I can dissolve it there as well.

John Mackey
Bentley College 2008

It is okay to be afraid. Not only is it OK . . . a little fear is probably good for you.

And the simple reason is: Fear leads to over-preparation. And when you over-prepare, *actual* failure becomes a much more remote possibility.

Savannah Guthrie
Hobart & William Smith Colleges 2012

There will be times in your life when knowing things won't matter as much as how scary the situation is.

And when that happens - you'll have to decide whether or not to get into the wheelbarrow.

Marc S Lewis
University of Texas at Austin 2000

Overcoming Fear

So why did I have a pit in my stomach?

Turns out that pit in my stomach was deep, abiding fear. But what was I afraid of?

So I looked directly at my fear and said "What's going on? Why are you here?" And fear said, "Don't worry about it! You're doing great!"

But I really grilled him, and finally my fear shrugged his shoulders and said, "I'm here because you're afraid of failing at comedy. Which, might I remind you, is the entire reason you moved to New York City in the first place."

Looking deeper into my fear revealed something I truly wanted.

And that precipitated a major course correction in my life.

And I looked at all of that fear and I said, "Thank you!" And it said, "No problem, man. That's what I'm here for."

And that's when I realized: Wow! If you let it, fear can become a kind of spirit guide on your path to a successful life.

Ed Helms
Knox College 2013

With curiosity comes fearlessness.

A child will walk up to a hot stove and touch it. Does it hurt? Yes! Was it a stupid thing to do? Well, kind of. But you have to admire the daring of that child.

His brave spirit is the angel inside each of us, the force that often seems to shrink as we grow bigger.

Steven Spielberg
University of Southern California 1994

There will be times when many of you will be tempted to play it safe . . .

I hope that, when you feel it in your heart, you will also take a leap of faith and go for it.

Katie Couric
Williams College 2007

You will inevitably make mistakes.

Learn what you can and move on.

At the end of your days, you will be judged by your gallop, not by your stumble.

Bradley Whitford
University of Wisconsin 2004

Overcoming Fear

You cannot let a fear of failure, or a fear of comparison, or a fear of judgement, stop you from doing the things that will make you great.

Charlie Day
Merrimack College 2014

Courage is the most important of all the virtues, because without courage you cannot be sure that you can practice any other virtue with consistency.

Maya Angelou
Smith College 1980

It's hard not to be afraid.
Be *less* afraid.

Susan Sontag
Vassar College 2003

Courage will be required of you on many fronts.

Have the courage to seek the truth, and speak the truth, to stand up for the underdog, and to stand up against intolerance.

Even if yours is the lone voice doing so.

Have the courage to trust your gut and your own moral compass - your innate understanding of right and wrong.

Have the courage to love fearlessly and unconditionally, and don't compromise that love because of arrogance or insecurity.

Katie Couric
Williams College 2007

Even at my lowest points when I agonized over not fulfilling other's expectations of me; or offending people whose approval I craved . . .

. . . my secret inner voice was always louder and stronger in the end than the ones that were telling me to be afraid.

Denise Di Novi
Simmons College 1997

Reframing
'Success' and 'Failure'

I left the cocoon of Harvard. I left the cocoon of Saturday Night Live. I left the cocoon of the Simpsons. And each time it was bruising and tumultuous.

And yet every failure was freeing, and today I'm as nostalgic for the bad as I am for the good.

So that's what I wish for all of you - the bad as well as the good.

Fall down. Make a mess. Break something occasionally.

Know that your mistakes are your own unique way of getting to where you need to be.

And remember that the story is never over.

Conan O'Brien
Harvard 2000

Accomplishment is unreliable.

"Succeeding", whatever that might mean to you, is hard, and the need to do so constantly renews itself. (Success is like a mountain that keeps growing ahead of you as you hike it).

And there's the very real danger that "succeeding" will take up your whole life, while the big questions go untended.

George Saunders
Syracuse University 2013

Making mistakes and being bad at something - this is how you get to be any good at all.

Savannah Guthrie
Hobart & William Smith Colleges 2012

Kindness! Which is absolutely crucial to living a good life.

Because, if you do everything else brilliantly but you don't do it with kindness, no matter how much you succeed, I believe you have failed.

Jehane Noujaim
Northwestern University, Qatar 2014

Whatever strong belief you now hold about what it means to be successful - I hope you will stay open to the possibility that you've got it all wrong, and graciously accept your new awareness, when it comes, with gratitude and humility.

Marc S Lewis
University of Texas at Austin 2000

I believe we're shaped by our failures, by our weaknesses and setbacks, at least as much as we are by our successes.

In many cases, those failures make ultimate success possible.

Terry Gross
Bryn Mawr College 2014

Think big for yourself. Dream big. But then, be ready to start small. In fact - that is exactly how it works.

You start small, and you work at the small thing like it IS the big thing.

That's how you GET the big thing.

Savannah Guthrie
Hobart & William Smith Colleges 2012

Don't be deceived by life's outcomes. Life's outcomes, while not entirely random, have a huge amount of luck baked into them.

Above all, recognize that if you have had success, you have also had luck - and with luck comes obligation.

You owe a debt, and not just to your Gods. You owe a debt to the unlucky.

Michael Lewis
Princeton 2012

I hope you'll make mistakes.

If you're making mistakes, it means you're out there doing something. And the mistakes in themselves can be useful.

Neil Gaiman
University of the Arts 2012

19

I beg you: don't buy society's definition of success. Because it's not working for anyone.

It's not working for women; it's not working for men; it's not working for polar bears; it's not working for the cicadas that are apparently about to emerge and swarm us.

It's only truly working for those who make pharmaceuticals for stress, sleeplessness and high blood pressure.

Arianna Huffington
Smith College 2013

Here's my last point about failure: Sometimes it's the best way to figure out where you're going. Your life will never be a straight path.

Denzel Washington
University of Pennsylvania 2011

In my experience, quite simply, success is happiness . . .

Happiness is success because, it turns out, happy people get jobs. Happy people create. Happy people win. Happy people fall in love and raise families. They lead and change the world.

Happy people are the ones who realize they don't actually need much more than they already have. And they appreciate what they've got.

Chris Sacca
University of Minnesota 2011

It really is better to fail than not to try, because if you never try, you'll never succeed. And as bad as failure feels, success feels so much better.

'Dr Ruth' Westheimer
Trinity College 2004

21

So why do I talk about the benefits of failure? Simply because failure meant a stripping away of the inessential.

I stopped pretending to myself that I was anything other than what I was, and began to direct all my energy into finishing the only work that mattered to me.

Had I really succeeded at anything else, I might never have found the determination to succeed in the one arena I believed I truly belonged.

I was set free, because my greatest fear had been realised, and I was still alive, and I still had a daughter whom I adored, and I had an old typewriter and a big idea.

And so rock bottom became the solid foundation on which I rebuilt my life.

J K Rowling
Harvard 2008

As a very successful woman, a single mother of three, who constantly gets asked the question "How do you do it all?" - for once I am going to answer that question with 100 per cent honesty here for you now.

The answer is this: I don't. Whenever you see me somewhere succeeding in one area of my life, that almost certainly means I am failing in another area of my life.

That is the trade-off. That is the Faustian bargain one makes with the devil that comes with being a powerful working woman who is also a powerful mother. You never feel a hundred per cent OK. You never get your sea legs. You are always a little nauseous. Something is always lost . . . Something is always missing . . .

Anyone who tells you they are doing it all perfectly is a liar.

Shonda Rhimes
Dartmouth College 2014

If you're going to fail, fail big.

If you don't, you're never going to make a difference . . .

Jerry Zucker
University of Wisconsin-Madison 2003

It took me a while to get it, but the hardest-working people don't work hard because they're disciplined. They work hard because working on an exciting problem is fun.

So after today, it's not about pushing yourself; it's about finding your tennis ball, the thing that pulls you.

It might take a while, but until you find it, keep listening for that little voice.

Drew Houston
Massachusetts Institute of Technology 2013

Failure. I have spent my life in a panic about it. That I'm not good enough. That I'm a fraud. That worth is measured in wins and losses.

But here is the thing - I hope you fail. All of you. I hope you fail miserably. . . Heroes can only come to life in the dark heart of failure.

Brad Falchuk
Hobart & William Smith Colleges 2014

It turned out that getting fired from Apple was the best thing that could have ever happened to me.

The heaviness of being successful was replaced by the lightness of being a beginner again, less sure about everything. It freed me to enter one of the most creative periods of my life.

Steve Jobs
Stanford 2005

Your biggest failure will happen if you go through life and never fail.

Because you'll never know what you could have done.

Steven Chu
University of Rochester 2013

We all stumble. We all have setbacks. If things go wrong, you hit a dead end - as you will - it's just life's way of saying time to change course.

This is what I do with every failure, every crisis, every difficult time. I say "What is this here to teach me?" And as soon as you get the lesson, you get to move on.

Oprah Winfrey
Stanford 2008

Freud in many of his great writings mentioned that part of the process of becoming an adult is learning to embrace failure; to accept it, to bounce back, to grow from it, and to use that to develop new and perhaps even obtainable goals.

I think the process begins by exploring yourself internally, and not going immediately outward.

James B Stewart
DePauw University 1989

The worst thing that can happen if you risk failure - is that you will fail.

But the fact is that most of the world's truly successful people fail many times over the course of a lifetime.

Michael Eisner
Denison University 1989

27

You will never make it.

That's the bad news, but the "shift" I invite you to make is to see it as fabulous, outstanding news.

For I don't believe there is actually an "it". "It" doesn't exist for an Artist.

One of the greatest gifts you can give yourself, right here, right now, in this single, solitary, monumental moment in your life – is to decide, without apology, to commit to the journey, and not to the outcome.

The outcome will almost always fall short of your expectations.

And if you're chasing that elusive, often deceptive goal, you're likely in for a very tough road.

For there will always be that one note that could have soared more freely; the one line reading that could have been just that much more truthful; that third arabesque which could have been slightly more extended; that one adagio which could have been just a touch more magical.

There will always be more freedom to acquire, and more truth to uncover.

As an artist, you will never arrive at a fixed destination.

This is the glory and the reward of striving to master your craft and embarking on the path of curiosity and imagination, while being tireless in your pursuit of something greater than yourself.

Joyce DiDonato
Juillard 2014

29

The things I've done that worked the best were the things I was the least certain about - the stories where I was sure they would either work, or more likely be the kinds of embarrassing failures people would gather together and talk about until the end of time.

Neil Gaiman
University of the Arts 2012

Success leads to the greatest failure, which is pride. Failure leads to the greatest success, which is humility and learning.

In order to fulfil yourself, you have to forget yourself. In order to find yourself, you have to lose yourself.

David Brooks
Sewanee University of the South 2013

Out of respect for things that I was never destined to do, I have learned that my strengths are a result of my weaknesses. My success is due to my failures.

Billy Joel
Fairfield University 1991

So, how do I define success?

Having a lot of money does not automatically make you a successful person. You want your work to be meaningful.

Because meaning is what brings the real richness to your life. What you really want is to be surrounded by people you trust and treasure, and by people who cherish you.

That's when you're really rich.

Oprah Winfrey
Stanford 2008

31

Famous 'Failures'

*Because, even those who are famous
and successful today once 'failed' –
some more than once!*

I've been waiting more than 30 years to say this, "Dad, I always told you I'd come back and get my degree" . . .

I'll be changing my job next year and it will be nice to finally have a college degree on my resume.

Bill Gates
Harvard 2007

32

Famous 'Failures'

People in general look at me as a successful ice-cream businessman, I think it's important to know that it would be just as true to look at me as a failure as a potter.

I spent six years of my life trying to become a potter. I love pottery, and I really wanted to become one, but I found that I enjoyed doing pottery a lot more than people liked buying my pots.

So I really wasn't able to make it as a potter.

Ben Cohen
Hampshire College 1990

Famous 'Failures'

I got it wrong a ton when I started out as a speechwriter for Hillary Clinton.

I got it wrong again when I became a presidential speechwriter. I worked on one speech about the financial system that caused the Dow to drop by 200 points.

So that speech could have been better, probably . . .

Jon Lovett
Pitzer 2013

Famous 'Failures'

And I started this path of stand-up and it was successful and it was great, but it was hard because I was trying to please everybody.

And I had this secret that I was keeping - that I was gay . . .

I finally decided that I was living with so much shame, and so much fear, that I just couldn't live that way anymore.

And I decided to come out and make it creative.

And I thought, "What's the worst that could happen? I can lose my career."

I did. I lost my career.

Famous 'Failures'

The show was cancelled after six years without even telling me; I read it in the paper.

The phone didn't ring for three years. I had no offers.

Nobody wanted to touch me at all.

Ellen Degeneres
Tulane University 2009

Surviving Challenges

Resilience . . .   You will inevitably face disappointment, loss, and struggles that are, at this moment, inconceivable and impossible to predict.

I want you to be prepared to reach down deep and find the inner fortitude you need after disappointments big and small, and the painful losses that are an inevitable part of life.

Katie Couric
Williams College 2007

When faced with the inevitable, you always have a choice.

You may not be able to alter reality, but you can alter your attitude toward it.

Margaret Atwood
University of Toronto 1983

Whatever blocks you encounter, you have learned that there is a way over, around or through them. It is not those obstacles that inhibit your progress but your confidence, and will to break the inertia of fear and doubt.

W Douglas Smith
DeVry University 2010

It is certain, if you aim high, that you will find your strongest beliefs ridiculed and challenged; principles that you cherish may be derisively dismissed by those claiming to be more practical or realistic than you.

But no matter how weary you may become in persuading others to see the value in what you value - have courage still. And persevere.

Madeleine Albright
Mount Holyoke College 1997

My favourite animal is the turtle. The reason is that in order for the turtle to move, it has to stick its neck out.

There are going to be times in your life when you're going to have to stick your neck out. There will be challenges and, instead of hiding in a shell, you have to go out and meet them.

'Dr Ruth' Westheimer
Trinity College 2004

By all reckoning, the bumblebee is aerodynamically unsound, and shouldn't be able to fly. Yet, the little bee gets those wings going like a turbo-jet, and flies to every plant its chubby little body can land on to collect all the nectar it can hold. Bumblebees are the most persistent creatures. They don't know they can't fly, so they just keep buzzing around.

Earl Baaken
University of Hawaii 2004

Every SEAL knows that under the keel, at the darkest moment of the mission, is the time when you must be calm, composed. When all your tactical skills, your physical power, and all your inner strength must be brought to bear.

If you want to change the world, you must be your very best in the darkest moment.

William McRaven
University of Texas 2014

With the understanding that you will face tough times and amazing experiences, you must also commit to the adventure.

Just have faith in the skills and the knowledge you've been blessed with, and go. Because regrets are born of paths never taken.

Michael Dell
University of Texas at Austin 2003

41

You cannot tell from appearances how things will go. Sometimes imagination makes things out far worse than they are; yet without imagination not much can be done.

Winston Churchill
Harrow School 1941

Learn humility and wisdom when you stumble, because it will help you when you succeed. Being forced to come back from that failure is why I'm standing here today.

Rahm Emanuel
George Washington University 2009

You can't make a cloudy day a sunny day - but you can embrace it and decide it's going to be a good day after all.

Jane Lynch
Smith College 2012

You should also know that there are external forces out there that are holding you back from really owning your success.

Studies have shown - and yes, I kind of like studies - that success and likeability are positively correlated for men, and negatively correlated for women.

This means that as men get more successful and powerful, both men and women like them better.

As women get more powerful and successful, everyone - including women - likes them *less*.

I've experienced this firsthand.

Do I believe I was judged more harshly because of my double-Xs? Yes.

Do I think this will happen to me again in my career? Sure.

I told myself that next time I'm not going to let it bother me, I won't cry. I'm not sure that's true. But I know I'll get through it.

I know that the truth comes out in the end, and I know how to keep my head down and just keep working.

Sheryl Sandberg
Barnard College 2011

You are now entering a world that's filled to the brim with idiots. Since there are so many idiots out there, you actually may start to think you're crazy. You are not. They are idiots.

Whatever you do, don't tell them that they are an idiot. There may come a day when you may need that idiot. Idiots may be idiots - but they do have a memory.

Lewis Black
University of California at San Diego 2013

44

The arc of history is longer than human vision. It bends. We abolished slavery, we granted universal suffrage. We have done hard things before.

And every time it took a terrible fight between people who could not imagine changing the rules, and those who said, "We already did. We have made the world new."

The hardest part will be to convince yourself of the possibilities, and hang on.

Barbara Kingsolver
Duke University 2008

Sometimes you find out what you are supposed to be doing - by doing the things you are not supposed to do.

Oprah Winfrey
Howard University 2007

And some of you - and now I'm talking to anyone who's been dumped . . . have not gotten the job you really wanted, or received those horrible rejection letters of grad school.

You know the sting of losing, or not getting something you badly want.

When that happens, show them what you are made of.

Jill Abramson
Wake Forest University 2014

Setbacks are inevitable. Just ask any successful person. You WILL screw up... and you will be let down. It's how you handle that adversity that will define who you are.

Katie Couric
Boston University 2011

BEING HUMAN(E)

You're only human, so learn to forgive yourself the little things, and do the best you can on the big things.

No-one is perfect, and expecting perfection from yourself, or anyone else, is a waste of time.

Callie Khouri
Sweet Briar College 1994

Taking a risk is not just about going for a job.

It's also about knowing what you know and what you don't know.

It's about being open to people and ideas.

Denzel Washington
University of Pennsylvania 2011

When you're the leader, it is really hard to get good and honest feedback, no matter how many times you ask for it.

One trick I've discovered is that I try to speak really openly about the things I'm bad at, because that gives people permission to agree with me - which is a lot easier than pointing it out in the first place.

To take one of many possible examples, when things are unresolved I can get a tad anxious . . . So I speak about it openly and that gives people permission to tell me when it's happening.

But if I never said anything, would anyone who works at Facebook walk up to me and say, "Hey Sheryl, calm down. You're driving us all nuts." I don't think so.

Sheryl Sandberg
Harvard Business School 2012

What I want to talk to you about today is the difference between gifts and choices. Cleverness is a gift. Kindness is a choice.

Gifts are easy - they're given after all. Choices can be hard. You can seduce yourself with your gifts if you're not careful, and if you do, it'll probably be to the detriment of your choices . . .

How will you use these gifts? And will you take pride in your gifts, or pride in your choices?

Jeff Bezos
Princeton 2010

We now communicate with everyone, and say absolutely nothing.

Ted Koppel
Duke University 1987

You can change the way you think about other people.

You can choose to see their humanity first - the one big thing that makes them the same as you, instead of the many things that make them different from you.

Melinda Gates
Duke University 2013

Exercise free will and creative, independent thought. Not for the satisfactions they will bring you, but for the good they will do others - the rest of the 6.8 billion, and those who will follow them.

And then you too will discover the great and curious truth of the human experience is that selflessness is the best thing you can do for yourself.

David McCullough Jr
Wellesley High School 2012

BEING HUMAN(E)

As you leave here, remember what you loved most in this place . . . I mean the way you lived, in close and continuous contact.

This is an ancient human social construct that once was common in this land.

We called it a community . . .

We danced. We participated.

Even when there was no money in it.

Community is our native state. You play hardest for a hometown crowd.

You become your best self.

You know joy.

Barbara Kingsolver
Duke University 2008

And have humility. Remember, the same people you pass on the way up are the ones who will catch you when you fall.

Because the truth is no-ones life is free of disappointments. Bad things do happen to good people.

Katie Couric
Trinity College 2014

As you're changing the world, never neglect family.

They're not just your foundation; they're the source of life's greatest fulfilment . . .

There's usually somebody else who can do your job but there's nobody else who can be a loving child or a devoted parent.

Susan Rice
Stanford 2010

You face certain traps in moving on from here. One ugliness of the 'real world' is its readiness to have you define your purpose in terms of an enemy. I'm talking about those we compete with or simply disagree with.

The purpose for far too many is less to build something better than to destroy the other side. No tactic is too low as long as you can get away with it.

More and more of public and private life seems defined by the strength of one's power rather than the strength of one's ideas. And it is surprisingly seductive, you'll find when you get out there. We all find victories easier to come by when they are about knocking others down instead of winning them over. But we also eventually find that these are empty satisfactions.

Atul Gawande
University of North Carolina 2014

54

Bond emotionally with friends, family, professional colleagues and those you interact with daily.

Understand that each of us is part of a web of relationships that is nurtured through love, kindness, compassion, empathy and joy.

Emotional bonds create effective teamwork, where nothing is impossible because you have a shared vision for service, contribution and success - and because you complement each other's talents and strengths.

Deepak Chopra
Hartwick College 2013

There are very few rules to improvisation, but one of the things I was taught early on is that you are not the most important person in the scene. Everybody else is.

And if they are the most important people in the scene, you will naturally pay attention to them, and serve them.

But the good news is - you're in the scene too. So, hopefully to them you're the most important person, and they will serve you.

No one is leading. You're all following the follower, serving the servant. You cannot win improv.

Stephen Colbert
Northwestern University 2011

Join the conspiracy, to be a class of people that rejects cynicism, that is not joining the ranks of the denizens of divisiveness or the nattering nabobs of negativity, but be lovers.

Join the conspiracy and love with all ot your heart and all of your courage.

Let your love be defiant. Let your love be rebellious.

Join the conspiracy and make change in your life because change will not roll in on the wheels of inevitability - it must be carried in on the backs of lovers.

Cory Booker
Stanford 2012

(On Nelson Mandela)

Because he was a man who understood that real change must come from within, who understood and incorporated the message of love and forgiveness that too many of us only give lip service to, he learned to love his jailers. And they, in turn, learned to love him.

They no longer saw each other as stereotypes, as people who came from different racial backgrounds; but they broke through the barriers that divide us, even in this country, to see each other in their full humanity.

Hillary Rodham Clinton
University of Illinois at Champaign-Urbana 1994

Imagine yourself in 50 years. You're in your early 70s, near the end of your career . . .

And you start to reflect on your life. You start to think of all your successes: your career successes, your family successes, the great memories that you've had.

But then you start to think about all of the things you wished you had done just a little differently, your regrets.

I can imagine what they might be.

You wish you had spent more time with your children; you'll wish that you had told your spouse how much you loved them more frequently; you'll wish you could have spent more time with, and told your parents how much you appreciated them before they passed away.

Salman Khan
MIT University 2012

Saint Francis, Buddha, Muhammad, Maimonides all spoke the truth when they said the way to serve yourself is to serve others.

And that Aristotle was right, before then, when he said the only way to assure yourself happiness is to learn to give happiness.

Mario Cuomo
Iona College 1984

We are not asked to do great things - we're asked to do all things with greater care.

Such an ideal is rare in a culture of so compromised values and so much cynicism. A culture that all too often knows the price of everything, and the value of nothing.

Martin Sheen
La Roche College 2013

For the longest time I thought that the test of my value was what I had to say.

When I wasn't talking, I did listen to others, but with half my mind figuring out what I'd say next.

To really listen takes active attention.

To have listened and absorbed the whole message, with all its connotations, its unspoken and maybe unintended shadings, makes it likelier that when you do speak, you will contribute more, and do so with fewer words.

John Walsh
Wheaton College 2000

You can validate others, empower others, and increase the net happiness, the positivity in the world.

Salman Khan
Rice University 2012

Since, according to me, your life is going to be a gradual process of becoming kinder and more loving: Hurry up. Speed it along. Start right now.

There's a confusion in each of us, a sickness, really: selfishness. But there's also a cure. So be a good and proactive, and even somewhat desperate patient, on your own behalf. Seek out the most efficacious anti-selfishness medicines, energetically, for the rest of your life.

George Saunders
Syracuse University 2013

The most important career decision you're going to make is whether or not you have a life partner, and who that partner is. If you pick someone who's willing to share the burdens and the joys of your personal life, you're going to go further.

Sheryl Sandberg
Barnard College 2011

Being Human(e)

People drop names to make themselves look more important.

They try to assert power, to make the world seem less terrifying.

They post pictures on Facebook to prove how "exciting" their lives are . . .

It's human nature to worry. Our tendency, as frail biological creatures, is to pretend to be bigger than we are.

Or to run away.

But I would ask you to fight this instinct.

Victor W Hwang
Austin Community College 2014

I highly recommend you all become members of the two H club: Hard work and Humility . . .

There is no substitute for hard work, for doing well at the job you're in.

So no matter how much potential you think you have, a little humility will serve you well - and help you focus on doing your best in the job you've got - rather than plotting to get the job you think you deserve.

Katie Couric
Williams College 2007

Always keep people in your life who don't quite understand what it is you do.

It'll keep you humble.   You're never as important as you think you are.

Jay Leno
Emerson College 2014

Staying True To You

I've learned that what you think about the world says less about the world than it does about you.

And when you show up in this world and have the courage to tell your truth in moments big - but more importantly, in moments small - then you are the architect, not only of your own destiny, but you're the architect of transformational change.

Cory Booker
Stanford 2012

We do not need magic to change the world.

We carry all the power we need inside ourselves already. We have the power to imagine better.

J K Rowling
Harvard 2008

Basically she (my mother) said to me:
"Well, it's ok if you're weird. Are you willing to pay the price for it?"

She said:
"You realize that not everybody is going to get you; not everybody is going to see what you see; not everybody's going to feel what you feel . . .

And not only may they not get it, they may not like you.

When it's all said and done, are you prepared to take that on, in order to stay an individual?"

Whoopi Goldberg
SCAD Savannah 2011

Know your true self.

Your true self is not your self-image that is dependent on the labels you and others have given yourself. Your true self is the innermost core of your being that is beyond all labels, definitions and limitations.

Deepak Chopra
Hartwick College 2013

Do not bow your heads. Do not know your place.

Defy the gods. You will be astonished how many of them turn out to have feet of clay.

Be guided, if possible, by your better nature.

Salman Rushdie
Bard College 1996

STAYING TRUE TO YOU

We each have our quirks.

Celebrate those, be goofy, tell corny jokes, dance awkwardly, express your half-baked thoughts - but most importantly laugh about your failures.

Chris Sacca
University of Minnesota 2011

So what's your story? What are you made of? What do you bring to the table? What excites you?

If you don't know who you are yet, that's okay. But start actively thinking about who you are, even if it feels a little weird.

Anders Holm
University of Wisconsin-Madison 2013

One of the greatest threats we face, simply put, is bullshit. We are drowning in it. We are drowning in partisan rhetoric that is just true enough not to be a lie . . .

But this is not only a challenge to society, it's a challenge we all face as individuals.

Life tests our willingness in ways large and small, to tell the truth. And I believe that so much of your future, and our collective future, depends on your doing so.

Jon Lovett
Pitzer 2013

If I can leave you with one thought . . . it's the idea that you can make a difference in this world. One individual - one child of light - can make a difference.

Norman B Rice
Whitman College 1998

Staying True To You

All external expectations, all pride, all fear of embarrassment or failure - these things just fall away in the face of death, leaving only what is truly important.

Remembering that you are going to die is the best way I know to avoid the trap of thinking you have something to lose.

You are already naked. There is no reason not to follow your heart.

Steve Jobs
Stanford 2005

Don't let your special character and values, the secret that you know and no one else does - the truth - don't let that get swallowed up by the great chewing complacency.

Meryl Streep
Vassar College 1983

If you doubt that a single person making a single decision can influence the future, think again . . . because that's almost all that ever does influence the future.

All of history is the accumulation of single decisions.

Barbara Kingsolver
DePauw University 1994

Soul is about authenticity.

Soul is about finding the things in your life that are real and pure. The things that are at your core.

The things you know you were put on this earth to do.

John Legend
University of Pennsylvania 2014

But the challenge of life I have found is to build a résumé that doesn't simply tell a story about what you want to be - but a story about *who* you want to be.

Because when you inevitably stumble and find yourself stuck in a hole, that is the story that will get you out.

What is your true calling? What is your dharma? What is your purpose?

Oprah Winfrey
Harvard 2013

Stay curious.

Don't miss the magic in life. Because it's all around you, if you keep your eyes open and your radar on.

Bill Whitaker
Hobart & William Smith Colleges 2008

Staying True To You

If you remember nothing else today, remember this: You are awesome.

I'm not suggesting you be boastful. No one likes that in men or women.

But I am suggesting that believing in yourself is the first necessary step to coming even close to achieving your potential.

Sheryl Sandberg
Barnard College 2011

Your life is precious. You've only got one.

Don't waste it on bad relationships, on bad marriages, on bad jobs, on bad people.

Waste it wisely on what *you* want to do.

Eric Idle
Whitman College 2013

Professional integrity begins with personal integrity.

You cannot get away with the idea "Our product has fewer defects than the competitor's" or "Our service is not as bad as others".

Relativism is not an option; it is all about honesty and loyalty. These are absolutes. Trust me, they will make your lives simpler - and they carry their own rewards.

Henry Kravis
Columbia Business School 2011

So to conclude my conclusion:

Follow your passion, stay true to yourself.

Ellen Degeneres
Tulane University 2009

Staying True To You

In film school, the first thing you study is character.

And you learn that insecure characters, characters that don't think much of themselves, are not very interesting. They aren't inspirational, or hopeful and no one wants to watch them. Ouch.

But the only characters worse than insecure characters are perfect characters. They are lifeless, boring, generic - they never feel authentic.

The best characters, the ones we love, who inspire us, who we want to remember forever, are flawed, and one-of-a-kind.

Jennifer Lee
University of New Hampshire 2014

There's that old joke, not very funny, that goes "No matter where you go, there you are." That's true.

The person who you're with most in life is yourself. And if you don't like yourself, you're always with somebody you don't like.

Marc S Lewis
University of Texas at Austin 2000

The moment that you feel that, just possibly, you're walking down the street naked, exposing too much of your heart and your mind and what exists on the inside, showing too much of yourself . . .

That's the moment you may be starting to get it right.

Neil Gaiman
University of the Arts 2012

Don't cut corners.
Don't B.S.
Don't lie.

Be proud of yourself and stand for something.

Money will come, trust me, but no amount of money in the world will help you sleep well at night if you haven't been legit.

Chris Sacca
University of Minnesota 2011

Being a good human being is more important than being good at my job . . .

If I don't feel my work has a higher purpose, or that my values and beliefs carry through in all aspects of my life, then I am failing at everything.

Denise Di Novi
Simmons College 1997

Don't sweat too much what other folks may think of you.

As Dr Seuss said, "Be who you are and say what you feel, because those who mind don't matter, and those who matter don't mind."

Susan Rice
Stanford 2010

Whatever path you take, whatever field or fields you choose to enter, the one constant you will find is that moral challenges await you.

At every step you will have to decide who you are. And who you are will change.

Lee Blessing
Reed College 2001

Every one of us has a calling. There is a reason why you are here.

I know this for sure, and that reason is greater than any degree. It's greater than any pay check.

And it's greater than anything anybody can tell you that are you *supposed* to do.

Your real job is to find out what the reason is - and get about the business of doing it.

Oprah Winfrey
Howard University 2007

Never be afraid to be different.

William Zinsser
Wesleyan University 1988

80

As soon as you have enough stuff, then you get to be - whatever - happy, fulfilled, at peace.

There's only one tiny flaw in that program. It doesn't work. Because you never have enough to be at peace.

So I'm going to propose something that will be a radical flip it here.

Start with who you are.

Let what you *do* be an expression of *who you are*.

And then you'll get whatever you get from the world.

John Jacob Scherer
Roanoke College 2010

Staying True To You

Life should be unpredictable.

And I'm very grateful that I never wasted any time trying to become somebody else's image of what I should be.

Jerry Zucker
University of Wisconsin-Madison 2003

Whatever it is that is calling to you, I urge you to ignore the voices that are telling you what you *ought* to do with your career and your family choices.

You cannot authentically live anyone's life but your own.

Gabrielle Giffords
Scripps College 2009

Trust, Intuition, and Being Present

When it comes to a decision between alternatives, we enumerate the cost and benefits and decide which one is better.

But there are times in our lives when the careful consideration of cost and benefits just doesn't seem like the right way to make a decision.

There are times in all of our lives when a reliance on gut or intuition just seems more appropriate. When a particular course of action just *feels* right

And interestingly I've discovered it's in facing life's most important decisions that intuition seems the most indispensable to getting it right.

Tim Cook
Auburn University 2010

Learn to check your ego at the door and start checking your gut instead.

Every right decision I've ever made has come from my gut.

And every wrong decision I've ever made was a result of me not listening to the greater voice of myself.

Oprah Winfrey
Stanford 2008

Don't worry about what your next line is.
Don't have any expectations.
And be in this moment.

Dick Costolo
University of Michigan 2013

Every one of us here has a chance to be truly happy.

Being present. We owe each other our full attention.

Why? It's because life is funnier when we're all laughing together, love is more intense, and we're all smarter when we're paying attention . . .

Being present is smarter, funnier and undeniably more attractive.

Chris Sacca
University of Minnesota 2011

Trust matters in a network world.
Trust is your most important currency.

Eric Schmidt
Carnegie-Mellon University 2009

Think to the moments in your life when you forgot to doubt yourself. When you were so inspired that you were just living and creating, and working.

Pay attention to those moments. They're trying to reach you through those lenses of doubt, and trying to show you your potential.

Jennifer Lee
University of New Hampshire 2014

The impact is what others frame for you and the world - *after* it happens.

The present is only what you're experiencing, and focused on, right now.

Dick Costolo
University of Michigan 2013

You have to have the courage to go with your gut and a willingness to take the smaller job.

Like life, in theater it doesn't pay to have a big ego. No jobs are too small for you.

If I didn't take the understudy position because I was too proud, or felt it was beneath me, I'm pretty sure I wouldn't be standing here in front of you today.

Say yes. Get coffee for people, run errands, make an impression as a hard worker - someone who is willing, when the opportunities arise for you, to show people what you've got, show them.

Who knows what'll happen?

Sutton Foster
Ball State University 2012

Do one thing at a time.

Give each experience all your attention.

Try to resist being distracted by other sights and sounds, other thoughts and tasks, and when it is, guide your mind back to what you're doing.

My warning is against distraction . . .

John Walsh
Wheaton College 2000

It's great to plan for your future. Just don't live there, because really nothing ever happens in the future.

Whatever happens, happens *now* - so live your life where the action is - now.

Jerry Zucker
University of Wisconsin-Madison 2003

I would like to suggest that our appetite for achievement in the personal and political realms must be balanced by an active non-doing. By love of and passion for the useless - for that which has no social or political utility or application.

It is in the realm of non-doing that we approach the counter pole to doing, which is Being, with a capital B.

Julius Lester
Hampshire College 1984

I wish you the ability to trust your instincts, follow your passions, and to find the ability to pursue a life where love of work and love of self are combined.

Annette Bening
San Francisco State University 1995

So paint in your mind the most grand vision; where you want to go in life.

Prepare, trust in, and execute on your intuition.

And don't get distracted by life's potholes.

Tim Cook
Auburn University 2010

Don't worry that you have no idea what to do next or, even if you do, don't get so married to that idea that you miss your 'aha' moments.

Get started but be very honest with yourselves: listen to your guts, take risks, be positive, don't be afraid of mistakes, keep learning and growing.

Omid Kordestani
San Jose State University 2007

When we forgive others, we free ourselves from the past and allow our hearts to be fully in the present moment, which is where love exists.

John Mackey
Bentley College 2008

When people show you who they are, believe them - the first time.

Oprah Winfrey
Wellesley College 1997

Remember:
Gut instincts are usually right.

M L Flynn
Hollins College 1995

Sometimes you have to take calculated risks and roll the dice, or risk growing old and having to say "I could have been . . ."

Michael Uslan
Indiana University 2006

And most important - have the courage to follow your heart and intuition.

They somehow already know what you truly want to become.

Everything else is secondary.

Steve Jobs
Stanford 2005

The Road
Less Travelled

Climb the mountain - not to plant your flag - but to embrace the challenge. Enjoy the air and behold the view.

Climb it so you can see the world, not so the world can see you.

Go to Paris to *be* in Paris, not to cross it off your list and congratulate yourself for being worldly.

David McCullough Jr
Wellesley High School 2012

Watch out, watch out as you go along, that what you're doing is not merely a job, not merely a career, but your work.

The thing that you really *want* to do.

Frances FitzGerald
Sarah Lawrence College 1982

95

Be hard on your beliefs. Take them out onto the verandah and hit them with a cricket bat. Be intellectually rigorous. Identify your biases, your prejudices, your privileges.

Tim Minchin

University of Western Australia 2013

Don't have a relationship with a partner who doesn't get it. You need a soulmate, not a cellmate.

Jay Leno

Emerson College 2014

The unfortunate, yet truly exciting thing about your life, is that there is no core curriculum. The entire place is an elective.

Jon Stewart

College of William & Mary 2004

You don't need a grand plan. Whatever plan you do have is probably going to change 100 times before you're 30 years old.

And you don't need to be an expert in something to try it.

Michael Bloomberg
University of North Carolina 2012

When I'm interviewing young people to work for me, I don't look at their transcripts.

I care if they're smart, literate, focused, and passionate about what they want to do. The ones who succeed are those who simply work harder and try harder than anyone else.

Denise Di Novi
Simmons College 1997

The best advice I'd been given over the years came from Stephen King twenty years ago.

His advice was this: "This is really great. You should enjoy it."

And I didn't. I wish I'd enjoyed it more.

It's been an amazing ride. But there were parts of the ride I missed, because I was too worried about things going wrong, about what came next, to enjoy the bit I was on.

Let go and enjoy the ride.

Because the ride takes you to some remarkable and unexpected places.

Neil Gaiman
University of the Arts 2012

Listen. Listening isn't passive.

It is an act of liberation that will connect you to the world with compassion, and be your best guide as you navigate the choppy waters of love, work and citizenship.

Bradley Whitford
University of Wisconsin 2004

Don't lose touch with your capacity to see absurdity, to laugh - including at yourselves - to enjoy, to take time out from striving.

And just be.

Elizabeth Drew
Reed College

THE ROAD LESS TRAVELLED

The wisdom of each generation is necessarily new.

This tends to dawn on us in revelatory moments, brought to us by our children . . . The world shifts under our feet. The rules change.

You'll make rules that were previously unthinkable . . .

Barbara Kingsolver
Duke University 2008

If you want to get ahead, volunteer to do the things no one else wants to do. And do it better.

Be a sponge. Be open and learn.

Bobbi Brown
Fashion Institute of Technology 2014

The Road Less Travelled

I made a spreadsheet. I listed my jobs in the columns and my criteria in the rows, and compared the companies and the missions and the roles.

So I sat down with Eric Schmidt, who had just become the CEO (of Google), and I showed him the spread sheet and I said, 'This job meets none of my criteria."

He put his hand on my spreadsheet and he looked at me and said, "Don't be an idiot."

Excellent career advice.

And then he said: "Get on a rocket ship. When companies are growing quickly and they are having a lot of impact, careers take care of themselves.

And when companies aren't growing quickly or their missions don't matter as much, that's when stagnation and politics come in."

If you're offered a seat on a rocket ship, don't ask what seat.

Just get on.

Sheryl Sandberg
Harvard Business School 2012

Believe that, if you make courageous choices, and bet on yourself, and put yourself out there - that you will have an impact as a result of what you do.

And you don't need to know now what that will be, or how it will happen.

Because nobody ever does.

Dick Costolo
University of Michigan 2013

It was the riskier road and, again, I could not have made a better decision.

Taking matters into my own hands changed everything. Led to everything. "Horrible Bosses," "Pacific Rim," "Saturday Night Live."

Creating the job, as opposed to having it offered to me, accelerated the process.

Draw your own conclusions here, but I think the lesson is obvious.

Don't wait for your break.
Make your break.
Make it happen for yourself.

Charlie Day
Merrimack College 2014

Be aware that - even before you have reached your ultimate professional destination - if you always strive for excellence, you can and should have a substantial impact on the world in which you live.

Sandra Day O'Connor
Gettysburg College 2008

Even if you're not yet an entrepreneur, you can be entrepreneurial in everything you do.

If you view each stop as an opportunity to learn something, there is always something you will take away from that experience.

Tory Burch
Babson College 2014

When you are not learning anything, it's time to move on. Move on, take a risk - even if you make big mistakes.

Because it is only through taking risks, and making mistakes that you learn.

The risks that I have taken have always taught me something important.

Jehane Noujaim
Northwestern University, Qatar 2014

We must remember that the marketplace does only one thing. It puts a price on everything.

The role of culture, however, must go beyond economics. It is not focused on the price of things, but on their value.

Dana Gioia
Stanford 2007

105

If you've really learned how to think, how to pay attention, then you will know you have other options.

It will actually be within your power to experience a crowded, loud, slow, consumer-hell-type situation as not only meaningful but sacred: on fire with the same force that lit the stars - compassion, love, the sub-surface unity of all things.

The only thing that's capital-T "True" is that you get to decide how you're going to try to see it.

You get to consciously decide what has meaning and what doesn't.

David Foster Wallace
Kenyon College 2005

If you want to be remembered for more than just the size of your income, or the square footage of your living space . . .

. . . seek to serve some good greater than your own.

Patrick Corvington
Hobart & William Smith Colleges 2011

Be brave enough to life live creatively.

The creative is the place where no one else has ever been.

Alan Alda
Connecticut College 1980

Do not live your life safely. I would take risks.

And do not do things just because everybody else does them.

Wilma P Mankiller
North Arizona University 1992

We are losing the fun race. How did that happen?

We are built for happiness, but we're doing something wrong.

No one takes vacations. No one unplugs. Ours has becoming a nation of overwork and under-agreement. So I'm asking you - Turn it around . . .

Chris Regan
Stanford 2007

If you have an idea of what you want to make - what you were put here to do . . .

. . . then just go and do that.

Neil Gaiman
University of the Arts 2012

You'll find that a mind set in its own ways, set in its ways locked down, is a mind and life wasted.

Don't do it.

Eric Schmidt
Carnegie-Mellon University 2009

What is the one sentence summary of how you change the world? Always work hard on something uncomfortably exciting!

Larry Page
University of Michigan 2009

Really there is no normal. There's only change, and resistance to it.   And then more change.

Meryl Streep
Barnard College 2010

Go   out   there   and   do   something remarkable.

Don't live down to expectations.

Wendy Wasserstein
Mount Holyoke College 1990

If you think about life in terms of what you are going to *do*, what you are going to *accomplish*, you're leaving out big parts of it.

Don't lose touch with your capacity to see absurdity, to laugh - including at yourselves - to enjoy, to take time out from striving, and just *be*.

Don't lose touch with your capacity to love. In fact, nurture it, for you will find that it is something that can grow. Let yourself need people, and let them need you. Don't forget to take time out to look at the trees.

If you do lose those things, you will have lost a great deal - and what are most commonly recognized by the outer world as accomplishments will have a certain emptiness.

Elizabeth Drew
Reed College

Be about more than money. Comfort and economic security are good, but they're not enough.

You should be about creating change, not just counting it.

Susan Rice
Stanford 2010

Have the courage to accept that you're not perfect.

Nothing is, and no-one is.

And that's OK.

Katie Couric
Williams College 2007

A Life of

Heart & Passion

You cannot draw any of your paths looking forward, so you have to figure out what you love to do – what you have conviction about. And go do that.

Dick Costolo
University of Michigan 2013

I know how tough this economy is for so many; how daunting it can be to find that first job; how difficult it can be to make your way in a job market that doesn't carry the promise of security anymore . . .

But even as you deal with that pressure, try not to let the search for security stop you from doing work that stirs you up; the kind of work you think about even when you're off the clock; the kind of work that you would do even if you weren't paid.

George Stephanopoulos
Franklin & Marshall College 2014

Take your idealism . . . the best of what you've learned here . . .

Take it with you out into the world. Cherish it. Nurture it. Never let it go.

Dan Glickman
Hobart & William Smith Colleges 2010

Go find your joy. Whatever that is, go find your joy.

Are you going to have a good day, or are you going to have a great day? Because it's completely up to you. It's what you're going to remember in the end.

You're not going to remember how you worried. You're not going to remember the what-ifs, or the whys, or who wronged you.

It's the joy that stays with you.

Sandra Bullock
Warren Easton Charter School 2014

115

Follow whatever your passion is.
Do something you love.

Michael Uslan
Indiana University 2006

The first thing to worry about: Will I marry well?   This is the most important decision you're going to make in your life.

If you have a great marriage and a crappy career, you will be happy. If you have a great career and a crappy marriage, you will be unhappy.

I tell university presidents that since the marriage decision is so central, they should have academic departments on how to marry.

David Brooks
Sewanee University of the South 2013

116

A LIFE OF HEART & PASSION

What you love can differ, but the love, once it comes, that feeling of waking up with a kind of eagerness, a crazy momentum that pushes you into your day, an excitement you realize you don't ever want to go way . . . That's important.

If you don't have that feeling, maybe you're lucky. You can lead a more sane life.

But if you do – I say congratulations. You have what it takes to begin.

Robert Krulwich
Berkeley Journalism School 2011

Being a celebrity has taught me to hide, but being an actor has opened my soul.

Meryl Streep
Barnard College 2010

First tell me what you love. And then tell me the most daring place to do it.

And then tell me if that place has a heart.

Diane Sawyer

University of Illinois at Champaign-Urbana 1997

Now when I say do what you love, I don't mean that you will love what you do every day. But for me, it was taking pictures and the arts that made me want to wake up in the morning .

If you do what you love, you will be a person that you LIKE. And since you have to spend more time with yourself than anybody else in the entire world, it is very important that you like yourself.

Jehane Noujaim

Northwestern University, Qatar 2014

One thing I came to realize after college was that the search for purpose is really a search for a place, not an idea. It is a search for a location in the world where you want to be part of making things better for others in your own small way . . .

It could be a classroom where you teach, a business where you work, a neighborhood where you live.

The key is, if you find yourself in a place where you stop caring - where your greatest concern becomes only you - get out of there.

Atul Gawande
University of North Carolina 2014

Is it enough just to have a passion?
It's not only enough. It's everything.

Neil Simon
Williams College 1984

119

Go forth with your careers, but leave space for your passions.

Remember that you are much, much more than a title or a bank account. You are dancers and poets, inventors and athletes, musicians and innovators.

If you give your passions room to breathe, you might find that is all they need to help you move the dial forward for everyone.

Salman Khan
MIT University 2012

I once interviewed a man who spent his whole life studying happiness, and he came back with this result.

Happiness is love, full stop.

David Brooks
Rice University 2011

A LIFE OF HEART & PASSION

Love what you do.

Get good at it.

Competence is a rare commodity in this day and age.

And let the chips fall where they may.

Jon Stewart
The College of William & Mary 2004

At the end of your life, you will never regret not having passed one more test, not winning one more verdict, or not closing one more deal.

You will regret time not spent with a husband, a child, a friend or a parent.

Barbara Bush
Wellesley College 1990

We don't beat the (Grim) Reaper by living longer. We beat the Reaper by living well and living fully, for the Reaper will come for all of us.

The question is: What we will do between the time we're born and the time he shows up? Because when he shows up it's too late to do all the things that you always want to kind of get around to.

Randy Pausch
Carnegie-Mellon University 2008

We have no choices in life when money is our motivational force. Our motivational force ought to be passion.

But this is lost from the moment we step into a system that trains us, rather than inspires us.

Erica Goldson
Coxsackie-Athens High School 2010

122

At the end of my final program with NBC, just before signing off, I said:

"Work hard, be kind, and amazing things will happen.

I have never believed that more.

Conan O'Brien
Dartmouth College 2011

The only way anybody succeeds is to love what he's doing. It doesn't mean it will be easily done.

It's picking out what you like to do that's sometimes the problem.

But doing what you want to do in your life is what your life is all about.

Malcolm Forbes
Syracuse University 1988

Service is better than selfishness, and usually a lot more rewarding.

Dr Gilbert, the Harvard happiness expert, has studies that prove that generous people are also happier people . . .

Keep caring about the environment, about politics, about women's rights, about the poor and disenfranchised, and, most of all, about others.

Katie Couric
Williams College 2007

Passion should be the fire that drives your life's work.

The key is to listen to your heart and let it carry you in the direction of your dreams.

Michael Dell
University of Texas at Austin 2003

Finding Your

Way Forward

Life isn't that complicated.

Tell the truth, be kind to people, and make sure not to do anything too stupid with your body - and things tend to work themselves out.

Brad Falchuk
Hobart & William Smith Colleges 2014

Do not focus your energies on making a living. That will come, I promise you. It will come almost as an accident, as a by-product, without your even having to think about it . . .

Bump around the scenery a bit, try new things and make mistakes and stretch your talents and make adjustments . . . Find every rich and satisfying thing, and it will still be okay in the end.

Gabrielle Giffords
Scripps College 2009

Sometimes the way to do what you hope to do will be clear-cut.

And sometimes it will be almost impossible to decide whether or not you are doing the correct thing.

Something that worked for me was imagining that where I wanted to be was a mountain. A distant mountain. My goal.

And I knew that as long as I kept walking towards the mountain I would be all right.

And when I truly was not sure what to do, I could stop, and think about whether it was taking me towards or away from the mountain.

Neil Gaiman
University of the Arts 2012

To get something you never had, you have to do something you never did.

Denzel Washington
University of Pennsylvania 2011

We rarely control the timing of opportunities, but we can control our preparation.

If you are prepared when the right door opens, then it comes down to just one more thing: Make sure that your execution lives up to your preparation.

Tim Cook
Auburn University 2010

Accept the world for what it is, and at the same time, make it your own.

Jane Lynch
Smith College 2012

128

I know this is hard to hear. But it's true: You're not ready for every big job and every opportunity. Not yet.

This is the point: It's NOT a good opportunity if you're not ready.

Savannah Guthrie
Hobart & William Smith Colleges 2012

Your assumptions are your windows on the world. Scrub them off every once in a while, or the light won't come in.

If you challenge your own, you won't be so quick to accept the unchallenged assumptions of others.

Alan Alda
Connecticut College 1980

I believe that if you can learn to focus on what you HAVE, you will always see that the universe is abundant, and you will have more.

If you concentrate and focus on what you *don't* have - you will never have enough.

Oprah Winfrey
Wellesley College 1997

The daily activity that contributes most to happiness is having dinner with friends.

The daily activity that detracts most from happiness is commuting.

Eat more. Commute less.

David Brooks
Sewanee University of the South 2013

Know that life is not fair and that you will fail often.

But if you take some risks, step up when the times are toughest, face down the bullies, lift up the downtrodden and never, ever give up . . .

If you do these things, then the next generation, and the generations that follow, will live in a world far better than the one we have today. And what started here will indeed have changed the world. For the better.

William McRaven
University of Texas 2014

Creativity is allowing yourself to make mistakes. Art is knowing which ones to keep.

Jerry Zucker
University of Wisconsin-Madison 2003

131

Remember that while there's certainly a lot wrong in the world today, there's also a lot right. Not everything needs changing. Some things need protecting – and that can be just as important, challenging, and rewarding as changing the world.

Mary Barra
University of Michigan 2014

All we need is for you to find joy in your journey; to find satisfaction in hard work; to be aware of what is happening around you; to free yourself from your imagined limitations; to listen, - and finally, to act - not to play make believe.

This isn't a television show. The choices are difficult and the consequences are real.

Bradley Whitford
University of Wisconsin 2004

132

Listen once in a while. It's amazing what you can hear. . .

Or sometime when you're talking up a storm so brilliant, so charming that you can hardly believe how wonderful you are - pause just a moment and listen to yourself.

It's good for the soul to hear yourself as others hear you. And next time maybe, just maybe, you will not talk so much, so loudly, so brilliantly, so charmingly, so utterly shamefully foolishly.

Russell Baker
Connecticut College 1995

Say yes to opportunity. Follow your instincts. Be eager and passionate. Keep learning. Nurture your real lasting relationships, and don't be a jerk.

Sutton Foster
Ball State University 2012

133

You study the most successful people and they work hard - and they take advantage of opportunities that come that they don't know are going to happen to them.

You cannot plan innovation. You cannot plan invention.

All you can do is try very hard to be in the right place - and be ready.

Eric Schmidt
Carnegie-Mellon University 2009

The problems of this world are solvable. Don't let anyone tell you differently.

The problems of this world are solvable - and they are solvable by the choices you make.

Patrick Corvington
Hobart & William Smith Colleges 2011

134

The world needs you before you stop asking naïve questions - and while you have the time to understand the true nature of the complex problems we face, and take them on.

Wendy Kopp
Boston University 2013

Everyone you will ever meet knows something you don't. Respect their knowledge and learn from them.

Bill Nye
University of Massachusetts 2014

Never stop learning. Education is a lifetime journey . . . Keep asking questions. Keep acquiring knowledge. Keep seeking truth.

Michael Bloomberg
University of North Carolina 2012

135

I feel very lucky to be standing here before you today. But it took me 19 years to get here.

Along the way, I have cried, and worried, and been passed over, disappointed and sometimes embarrassed. I have been heartbroken.

And I have been overjoyed, and proud, and challenged, and tickled and awestruck.

Do you know what I really wish I would have told that girl way back when?

"Enjoy all of it.
It is a blessing to be alive."

Savannah Guthrie
Hobart & William Smith Colleges 2012

A career is not something that you put on like a coat. It is something that grows organically around you, step-by-step, choice-by-choice, and experience-by-experience.

Everything adds up. No work is beneath you. Nothing is a waste of time unless you make it so.

Wade Davis
Colorado College 2010

They say that you're the average of the 5 people you spend the most time with. Think about that for a minute: who would be in your circle of 5?

One thing I've learned is: surrounding yourself with inspiring people is now just as important as being talented or working hard.

Drew Houston
Massachusetts Institute of Technology 2013

One of the most important decisions you will make in your life is who you choose to surround yourself with.

When you are out there taking the big risks, you need friends and family to help you when you fall.

When you feel like you have made all the wrong decisions, they will help you laugh at yourself and pick you up off the floor.

They are equally important when you succeed, because they will keep you humble and grounded.

Friends are the family you get to choose. They are the people you will come back to for support with all your successes, as well as your failures. Nurture and treasure them.

Jehane Noujaim
Northwestern University, Qatar 2014

Most of my own life, I thought I had to choose between a safe route and the adventurous . . .

I believe that you can have both: security and adventure.

Bread on the table while taking your shots at the moon.

The revolutions of our generation are not being catalyzed by generals, or politicians...

but by highly empowered individuals like yourselves - the wizards of our time so speak - who can see with clarity how the assumptions of previous generations no longer apply.

Salman Khan
MIT University 2012

Life is difficult, and complicated, and beyond anyone's total control.

And the humility to know that will enable you to survive its vicissitudes.

J K Rowling
Harvard 2008

It took me a long time of standing still and being quiet to figure out what in retrospect appears to be a pretty simple lesson: writing a novel and living a life are very much the same thing.

The secret is finding the balance between going out to get what you want, and being open to the thing that actually comes your way.

Ann Patchett
Sarah Lawrence College 2006

How to Deliver a Great Speech

Whether it's Graduation, or any other event, here are some points on producing a speech that people will actually want to listen to

There are some truly great and insightful graduation speeches that have stood the test of time. They still inspire because they pass on nuggets of hard-earned wisdom, while at the same time being interesting and entertaining. They engage their audience.

The great ones fill your heart with warmth and hope, and connect you to their speaker. They resonate. They inspire. They are the rare ones.

And then there are the others. Most speeches are pretty much instantly forgotten. Usually they fade because they are as exciting as tapioca, and bore their listeners into disconnection. For the true horrors, obscurity is just wishful thinking; the worst of them have attained immortality by redefining tedium.

Top Tips for Speakers

Having spent hundreds of hours listening to and reading thousands of speeches – it's been interesting to be able to form an overview.

It quickly becomes obvious what makes a winner. And what does not.

If you're about to write a graduation speech – or any other speech come to think of it – here are some observations.

If you do take the time to read these, your audience will be endlessly grateful.

1 - *It's really not about you. Honestly, really, truly - no-one out there wants to hear your life story. A graduation day is full of excitable kids and their relieved parents. It's their day. They want to know what it is you have to offer them. What can you say that will help them to lead a better life?*

Top Tips for Speakers

2 - *Be generous. Instead of reinforcing how important and successful you have become, give them something important that life has taught you. Something that will really make them reconsider the status quo, and show them how they can enhance their lives.*

3 - *Share meaningfully. Throughout all your successes, what are the things that are really closest to your heart? What has sustained you? What has the most meaning for you? Why not pass that insight on . . .*

4 - *It's not a biography lesson. (To reinforce #1 above) Presumably if you've been asked to speak you've had a level of success in some arena - however, the very worst and most boring speeches are the backstory: a chronological list of events and accomplishments. They always end up being ego-ridden and dry, dry, dry. If you want them to listen, keep it interesting. Generally what interests people most - is hearing about them, not you.*

Top Tips for Speakers

5 - It's not a political rally. If you work in the corridors of power, chances are everyone already knows your stance. Please don't squander this opportunity to add real value to someone's life by reinforcing, or even worse, justifying your own position.

6 – Keep it light. You've been invited to talk at a day of celebration. So make your words celebratory. Yes, there may be a lot wrong with the world but this is not the time to dwell on that. Keep focussed on the up-side.

7 – Keep it human. The best speakers connect with their audience through the heart. The way to do this is to show them you're human too. Share something that lets them know that.

8 - Reframe 'success'. Not all success is quantifiable on the world stage, at the top of the corporate ladder, or within a bank vault. What has your journey through life taught you? Has it changed what 'success' really means to you now?

9 - Don't only talk about success. Not everyone's life will pivot around 'success'. But it's still possible to live a meaningful life. Be inspiring, but not judgmental or confining.

10 – Include Failure. Everyone's life has some. It's the reality of failures and stuff-ups and flaws that make a person interesting, and often more compassionate and nicer to know. Sharing some of yours (even if they're rare) will help you to connect with everyone, and make you much more human and approachable. It will also make you an inspiring example of how you can go on to be a success despite having 'failed' earlier on.

11 – Don't add pressure. There's already enough of that around. Everyone listening to you has the opportunity to 'change the world' but, if that's your focus, frame it as an enticing opportunity. Offer an invitation rather than delivering an obligation. People respond better to enticement than directives.

Top Tips for Speakers

12 – Create stories. Bring the important points you want to highlight alive. Tell a (brief) story to make them real. And interesting. And memorable.

13 – Make 'em laugh. If you can, it always helps. Nothing makes the human heart warm more than laughter. It doesn't have to be stand-up – wryness and wit work well too. Self-deprecation always hits the mark.

14 – Make 'em want more. A good speech is a brief speech. Keeping them interested, laughing and there for only a short time will make you well-liked, well-received and well-remembered. The perfect guest speaker in fact!

Look Who's Talking

Here are some of the people who have been talking to you. Many names you'll recognise instantly, some maybe not. Either way, they're all included in this book not only because of the success they've achieved, but because they have something to offer you.

Also available:

for more details, and many more quotes:

www.graduationinspiration.com